My Marie Curie Journey

Christine Murphy

Published by Christine Murphy
Printed by Biddles 2020

Biddles
Castle House,
East Winch Rd,
Blackborough End,
King's Lynn,
Norfolk
PE32 1SF

A catalogue record for this book is available from the British Library.
ISBN 978-0-9934175-7-3

Typeset in Calibri 12pt by re:creates
Cover photography and design by Christine Murphy and re:creates
Printed in Great Britain.

Contents

Foreword

For residents of Solihull, Marie Curie is a way of life! As soon as we moved here, we became aware of the many small-scale events seeking to separate us from the odd 50p or the occasional fiver to raise funds for Marie Curie Centre Warren Pearl.

We marvelled at the many and various schemes, some mundane, some ingenious, some bizarre, thought up by our fellow Silhillians to raise money for this charity which seemed to be woven into the fabric of the Borough. The pages which follow will introduce you to Christine Murphy, the driving force behind many of these ideas and also the 'connector in chief' who brought all these elements together.

The new hospice, opened in 2013, is a monument to the residents of Solihull; we've each paid for a brick. We each know someone who has benefited from our generosity. A school friend of mine, Chris Boyle, spent his final months in the new hospice; I visited him there at least once a week, usually on my bike [nurses go mad for Lycra you know]. Chris was cared for with compassion and love and departed this life with dignity. So many of the hospice staff were present at his funeral.

My thirteen-year-old Grandson, Noah Maclean, recently climbed Snowdon. Completely off his own bat he decided to get himself sponsored and where did the money go? All £300+ to Marie Curie – it's in our DNA.

This book is not just a tribute to a hospice and its community, it's also a valuable slice of social history and an instruction manual for fund raisers everywhere – may they read and learn!!

Don Maclean

Introduction

It has been said that everyone has a story to tell. What motivates the telling of that story can vary from person to person.

My Marie Curie journey started in 1992 when I took up the post of Centre Fundraising Manager where I remained for twelve years. This book is intended to describe the journey from Marie Curie Memorial Foundations 'Warren Pearl House' in Warwick Road, Solihull, to the magnificent state of the art Marie Curie Hospice West Midlands just around the corner in Marsh Lane, Solihull. More importantly, it offers the opportunity to write about the wonderful team of people with whom I had the privilege of working during my Marie Curie Years.

To steal a quote from one of my favourite films *It's a Wonderful Life*; "Each person's life touches so many other lives." I have had the privilege of seeing the Marie Curie palliative teams in action both in the hospices and in the community where patients have chosen to die at home. It was, indeed, a privilege to work alongside a wonderful team of people both within and working alongside our fundraising team. Friendships made at Marie Curie were very special indeed.

When I took up the post of Centre Fundraising Manager at the Marie Curie Hospice in Solihull, known as Warren Pearl, part of my job included going out into the community and talking about the hospice. Much to my surprise, it soon became apparent that in 1992 the local community, although having a fondness for the place, did not appreciate this it was in fact a charity and that the charity is Marie Curie Cancer Care. The sign outside the building in Warwick Road changed from Warren Pearl House, to Marie Curie Centre Warren Pearl. Then, as time went on, people had a greater understanding of the work of palliative teams and were less afraid of the word 'hospice'. So, the sign changed to Marie Curie Hospice

Solihull. Of course, the new state of the art hospice in Marsh Lane is known as the Marie Curie Hospice West Midlands.

One thing that does not change is the care. A simple act of caring creates endless ripples.

Christine Ann Murphy

Former Marie Curie Centre Warren Pearl
Fundraising Manager

What's in a name?

The Marie Curie International Memorial was formally established on 6 July 1948, and shortly afterwards became the Marie Curie Memorial Foundation.

Around the same time, fundraising for the new charity started when Mrs. Alice Macpherson donated her diamond engagement ring, which sold for £75. The foundation then launched an appeal, bringing in £4,000, and Marie Curie's daughter Eve gave permission to use her mother's name.

Working with the Queen's Institute of District Nursing, the charity's inaugural committee launched a joint national survey to investigate the needs of cancer patients and the best ways of helping them. The detailed report set the direction for work in the early years. The first Marie Curie Home for cancer patients was opened in 1952, based in an old National Trust property called the Hill of Tarvit in Cupar, Fife. The ground floor apartments contained a collection of furniture, paintings and porcelain, which were kept open to the public, in return for rent set at £1.

During the 1950s and early 1960s, the charity opened nine more Marie Curie Homes in adapted buildings. They were; Tidcombe Hall, Tiverton (1953), Edenhall, Hampstead (1954), Strathclyde House, Glasgow (1954), Conrad House, Newcastle upon Tyne (1957), Sunnybank, Liverpool (1959), Holme Tower, Penarth (1959), Harestone, Caterham (1961), Ardenlea, Ilkley (1963), Belfast Home, Belfast (1965) and...Warren Pearl House, Solihull (1965).

Warren Pearl House comprised three properties; 909-911 Warwick Road, Solihull, which were purchased, from Windylow Preparatory School, by Marie Curie Memorial Foundation. The properties were probably built around the turn of the century as spacious private houses. When bought, the classrooms and cloakrooms were still in situ. Plans to develop 909 Warwick Road as staff residential quarters and an administrative and training block were not pursued owing to the current lack of funds, at the time, and the house was subsequently sold in 1969 to the West Midlands School of Bridge. Warren Pearl Marie Curie Centre opened in 1965 and was joined at ground floor level by a connecting corridor.

The name Warren Pearl was chosen because Amy Warren Pearl, wife of surgeon Frank Warren Pearl, was a benefactor of the charity. Amy Warren Pearl's survival from the sinking of the Lusitania prompted her to devote her life to charitable works. She was one of the founding members of the Marie Curie Memorial Foundation. Over the years there were extensive alterations and improvements so the property was very different during my Marie Curie years than that acquired in 1965.

What's in a name? Warren Pearl House became Warren Pearl Marie Curie Centre. It was then renamed Marie Curie Centre Warren Pearl. The name change was deemed necessary so that the charity's name would take precedence in the title. The new, state of the art, hospice which opened in 2014 is now called Marie Curie Hospice West Midlands which reflects the nature and geographical coverage of the work undertaken by this remarkable place.

My first visit to Warren Pearl

Following an advertisement for a Marie Curie Fundraiser I met with Mrs. Barbara Hampel, who needed an assistant to help her cover the whole of Warwickshire and Birmingham as a fundraising manager. Barbara, a native Scot and proud of it, put her heart into her fundraising for Marie Curie Cancer Care. Although she could have easily employed me as her assistant, she saw the potential which would benefit the charity. The Marie Curie Cancer Care needed a fundraiser for their Centre in Solihull, so Barbara suggested that I have an informal interview with the Matron to decide whether I wanted to apply for the post.

I arrived at 911-913 Warwick Road, Solihull, and saw the sign which read 'Warren Pearl House'. As I walked through the door for my first visit to Warren Pearl, the reception area was to the right and not immediately obvious. As I entered the building my eyes were drawn to the notice board on the right. Ahead I saw an old-fashioned lift with concertina doors, it was the type of lift one would see in a very old-fashioned department store. The sliding window in reception to my right opened and the smiling face of Sue Bodfish appeared. She politely and cheerily asked me if she could help. I explained I had come for an informal interview with the Matron, Miss Sally Derry. Sue then telephoned the Matron and was asked to escort me to her room.

Parts of the building certainly had a feel of being in a boarding school and I was now being escorted to the Headmistresses room! However, Miss Sally Derry, Matron of the Centre, had the warmth of a caring nurse combined with competency and efficiency. After this informal chat I was completely smitten with the idea of working for this hospice. I put forward my application and was called for interview by a panel comprising: Miss Sally Derry, Mrs. Dorothy Dare, volunteer, Mr. Mike Thorne Head of Fundraising, and Mrs. Barbara Hampel, Regional Fundraising Manager.

I was offered the post of Centre Fundraiser and started my journey in November 1992. Like any fundraiser worth their salt, I had done my homework in advance of taking up my post. Safeway's Supermarket was opening a store on the same day I started work for Marie Curie Cancer Care. I had drafted a letter to the Manager of that store which began "I am writing to you on the first day in my new job to wish you well on the first day in your new job and I hope, as neighbours, we can work together."

I asked permission to use the computer in the General Office but was told, by the Matron, that I had to do a week's induction and that had to take priority. I explained that the letter had to be sent on my first day and she understood the importance and offered me the use of a typewriter until the computer for the fundraising department arrived. She emphasised the importance of the induction as it was clear I intended to 'hit the ground running'. She was a very wise woman.

That induction week proved to be invaluable as I met every manager in the Centre and had the opportunity to spend time with them and their staff. Time was also well spent finding my way around the labyrinth which was Warren Pearl. Taking the stairs on the right of the reception area, the first landing was the nurse's station where they met for briefing meetings.

Following the steps to the left took me into the wards which were named after precious gems; Diamond 4 beds, Sapphire 6 beds, Jade 3 beds, Emerald 5, Crystal 1, Topaz 1, and Opal 1. The staff and volunteers were, in my opinion, all precious gems!

Warren Pearl Staff

It was such a pleasure being introduced to the staff at Warren Pearl during my induction. Having found my way around Warren Pearl which was, indeed, a warren, I learned how a building which was originally a boarding school, had been adapted to accommodate a hospice. This is my description of the building as I knew it from 1992-2004.

It seems strange to describe a building which no longer exists but it feels perfectly natural to describe a building which was the forerunner to the purpose-built state of the art building. Warren Pearl was not purpose built but every inch was used for the maximum benefit of the patients and staff. A year after Sally Derry arrived a ramp to the main entrance was built and automatic doors were installed. The reception area was refurbished and other changes were made to make the reception area was more obvious to visitors and much more practical for the staff.

If I take you through the main entrance, past the reception, there was an old-fashioned lift ahead with concertina doors like old department stores used to have. On the right there were stairs leading to the wards and the relatives' sitting room. Turn left from the lift and you would find a small office housed the volunteer manager. Further down the corridor you would find Day Care on the left, which was opened by Duchess of Gloucester, and on the right patients' hairdressing room, aromatherapy room and a bathroom.

Further along the corridor there was a lounge and a conservatory. From the lounge, bearing left into a corridor, which connected the two buildings, led to the kitchen and catering staff door on the right. Further on from the kitchen and turning left there was the original front door to one of the buildings. In that short corridor on the left was the Matron/Centre Director's office and on the right two rooms which were originally used as staff dining and sitting rooms.

The flight of stairs next to the sitting room led to the first floor where the administration, finance and education offices were. It was on this floor that a very small office was, initially, allocated to fundraising. Up to the next flight of stairs were three rooms; the nurse's changing room, right next to the Home Care Team room and across the landing the room in which I was interviewed.

It was not long before there were changes to the location of the fundraising office and the education offices, as both teams were outgrowing their rooms. The fundraising office moved to the top floor into the room where I was first interviewed. The Education Department took back the small room we were using and benefitted from more space. Our fundraising team took great pride in not just raising money but saving money. So, when we moved, we had all the office furniture donated from one of our corporate sponsors, not just for fundraising but for the Centre Director's office and all the staff.

Going back through the corridor which joined the two buildings, and returning to the reception area, by turning right you would take yourself up to the nurses briefing room, a small upstairs kitchen, the relatives' sitting room and the wards, which were named after precious gems. I had the privilege of working with some very special 'gems', namely the staff and volunteers at Marie Curie Centre Warren Pearl.

Sally Derry, Matron and latterly Centre Director, oversaw everything from finance to the fir trees in the gardens. Sally worked closely with various Medical Doctors over the years, namely Dr. Ben Hill, Dr. Ian Morgan, Dr. Mark Sterry, Dr. Samira Gabra, Dr. Catherine Gearing and Dr. Goode. Besides caring for the patients in Warren Pearl, the medical team was involved in lecturing students, junior and senior hospital doctors and assessing patients in local

14

hospitals, either to give advice on management or prior to them being admitted to Warren Pearl.

Sally Derry took a great interest in the staff she managed and had a great rapport with the volunteers. From January 1992, until her retirement in 2000, Sally managed the following Unit Sisters; Ellen Ralphs, Kay Horton, Laura Joy and Sarah Clemett. Each morning Sally would go up onto the wards and, depending on the duty rota, would meet the Night Staff before they left and the Day team when they arrived. The Nursing Team was made up of the Unit Sister, who was supported by Senior Staff Nurses. They, in turn, lead teams of other Staff Nurses and Nursing Auxiliaries. They all worked very closely within the highest standards of care for patients.

During my time at Warren Pearl, the Home Care Team comprised four initially; Anne Hardie, Angela Hastwell, Linda Bailey, Jane Watson; then later, Jane Watson, Mary Fisher, Charm Kelso and Chris Cheadle. The Home Care Team, of Marie Curie nurse specialists, at Warren Pearl provided support and advice for patients and their carers within their own homes. They worked primarily within the community, together with the GP and District Nurses, they strived to enable patients to stay at home whenever possible. The team encouraged patients to live life to the full and were helped to face an uncertain future.

The roles of Occupational Therapist and the Physiotherapist are closely linked with the ultimate aim of improving quality of life for both the individual and their carer. Jo Bray was the first Occupational Therapist I had the pleasure of meeting in 1992. Over the years, the Day Care, Physiotherapy, and Occupational Therapy have been supported by the following people; Nikki Goodyear, Marion Dowding, Jackie Millichap, Christine Brown, Linda Thompson, Claire Pritchard, Samantha Cox, Claire Evans, and Staff Nurses Rachel Lockwood and Veronica Moore.

My induction week included time spent in Day Care. Head of Day Care at the time, Jo Bray, showed a great interest in supporting Fundraising. The Day Care patients were always pleased to see someone from Fundraising and were delighted to be part of the first fundraising initiative in December 1992, 'The Wishing Tree'.

I am delighted to say that many of the staff, despite being retired, have kept in touch. Cathy Gurney, Bereavement Services Co-Ordinator, Joan Griffin, Day Care Volunteer and former Physiotherapist Marion Dowding are part of the Marie Curie Walking Group. Cathy was the Bereavement Services Co-Ordinator and after four years in post, she had a team of 18 volunteers. Those volunteers were able to offer bereavement care to the family and friends of patients who have been cared for by Marie Curie Centre Warren Pearl. Cathy worked very closely with Solihull Bereavement Counselling Service.

The Pastoral Services Team comprised, Father Ted Simpson, Rev. George Hodkinson, Rev. Wilkinson, Rev. Nora Saunders, and Brother Andrew. The work of a Chaplain is a ministry of listening, and of helping patients and their carers to draw on whatever gives them strength. I know that we in the Fundraising Team certainly drew our strength from our Christian faith.

The Education Department over the years welcomed the following people:

Gwyneth Morgan (Tutor), Lyn Rogers (Assistant), Sharon Hudson (Staff Development Officer), Kay Thorman (Staff Development Officer), Simon Chippendale (Nurse Lecturer), Dion Smyth (Nurse Lecturer) and Christine Lake (Secretary). Melanie Carthy and Jane Bartholomew (Staff Development Officers). It was the Nurse Lecturer's responsibility for developing, delivering and managing professional education programmes based at Warren Pearl. The Education Department worked very closely with the Staff Development Officers. The role of the Staff Development Officer involved ensuring that all staff and volunteers received up to date and thorough training in all aspects of their work, in order to develop their practical, professional and interpersonal skills.

When I arrived in 1992 Carol Seale was Matron's PA, Molly Tick was the Finance Officer and Sue Bodfish was Head Receptionist. When Molly retired, Liz Hancock took on the role of Finance Officer. When Carol left to go to University, Christina Barrett became Matron's PA. Sue Bodfish went on to become Volunteer Services Manager with John Bendell.

Staff were always given opportunities to change roles and develop in order to fulfil their potential and serve the patients best interests. Indeed, in 2000 Liz Hancock became Non-Clinical Services Manager, responsible for the smooth running of administration, finance, payroll, domestic, maintenance and catering services. Carol Entwistle-Smith, the Services Manager, was responsible for managing all catering activities within the Centre. The Catering Team and the Domestic Team known as 'The Pink Team' reported directly to Carol.

As the work of Centre Director seemed endless, Sally employed a House Manager. Mike Witts was the first House Manager who responsible for keeping the old former preparatory school in good order and managing the handymen, Tony Pettit and John Quinsey. When Mike Witts retired, John Rogers took on the role of House Manager.

Volunteer Services Department

When Chris Seaton and I organised our first Daffodil Campaign in 1993, Eric Francis, Volunteer Services Manager, was only too pleased to help. When Eric retired, John Bendell took on the role. As the volunteer base grew it soon became too much for one person, so Jeff Sutton joined John. When Jeff moved Sue Bodfish and John Bendell worked together.

Centre Fundraising Team

I took up a full-time post as Centre Fundraiser in 1992. In 1993 Chris Seaton took a part time secretarial post. We were then joined by Sue Noone who came to help with the collection box placements. Julia Jones came to help at Centre Fundraising, and was then promoted and took up an Area Fundraising Manager post. Liz Earls was the Manager of the Warren Pearl Shop and she was then promoted to Administration Manager for the Midlands. Martin Bishop came to support Centre Fundraising and left to take up a Fundraising post in London.

It soon became apparent that the Finance Department in the Centre could not cope with the money coming in from Fundraising so it was decided that Fundraising should have a Finance Officer. At this point our esteemed volunteer, Horace Gillis, stood in until a full-time Finance person could be found. Horace had a great deal of experience in finance advised that the new Fundraising Finance Officer should only deal with finance. It was very wise advice because our whole team were multi-tasking most of the time. Pat Kirtland joined us as Finance Officer and enjoyed contributing to the work of fundraising and joined the team in supporting the events after work.

The events and activities were growing fast, and although we had fantastic support from volunteers, we needed full time administration support so Sue Anderson came to job share with Chris Seaton to provide full-time support. Pat took time off to have an operation and, during that time, Carole Seale took up the role during a break from university. Carole had been Matron's PA before Christina Barrett. Pat only returned to work for a short time before handing in her notice. Sheila Swarbrick then came to join us as Finance Officer and, during that time, she married John and became Sheila Hills.

18

The fundraising events and administration were growing fast and we were all working at full capacity when Head Office announced that The Centre Fundraising Team would also cover Warwickshire. So, after talking to the Chairman Sir Nicholas Fenn, it was decided that an Assistant could be employed to help with Warwickshire. Christine Lake, originally in the Education Department, came to join the team when we were fundraising for Marie Curie Centre Warren Pearl & Warwickshire. When Christine left, Chris Seaton, Sue Noone, Sheila Hills, Sue Anderson and I continued with the wonderful support of volunteers.

Although the Centre Fundraising Team was managed by, and reported to, the Director of Fundraising in London, Sally took the team under her wing and into her heart. As Fundraising Manager, I was included in the Heads of Department Meetings that Sally chaired. This afforded me the opportunity to be fully informed of the work and the needs of the Centre whilst out in the community.

Putting the Fun into Fundraising

The Marie Curie Memorial Foundation was a pioneer of direct-mail fundraising – writing to potential donors and asking them for support. Appeals were backed by popular celebrities at the time.

In the late 80's/early 90's, Community Fundraising was introduced with fundraisers covering every region of the country and, in addition, Centre Fundraisers for each Marie Curie hospice.

The early days

I was offered the post of Centre Fundraiser and started my journey in November 1992. I was shown to my compact office which had a kitchen chair and filing cabinet and a table with a leg missing. That was not the only thing missing. There was the obvious absence of a telephone and computer. The first amount of money raised was

19

from BT for not installing the telephone on time! I had to use the typewriter in the General Office until my computer arrived. Marie Curie Centre Warren Pearl was not purpose built but every effort was made to maximise the space available. As the fundraising grew, the Fundraising Department moved from the second floor in a very small office to the top floor in a much bigger office. Carrying display boards, and various promotional items down three flights of stairs kept us all fit! We didn't need gym membership in those days.

The Director of Community Fundraising, Mr. Mike Thorne, did everything he could to support and encourage the newly appointed Fundraising Managers. Meetings with Marie Curie fundraisers were organised and information sharing proved most worthwhile. One of my fundraising colleagues suggested that I contact the Sales Director of an exhibition company at the NEC which was 'on my patch'. The Sales Director referred me to his manager and, as a result of my meeting with the Manager of Giltspur Show Props (later known as PO Exhibition Services and later still known as Melville Exhibition Services) this exhibition company supported Marie Curie Cancer Care for over 14 years. The management and staff put their heart and soul into making each special event extra special.

I inherited two fundraising events, namely The Warren Pearl Christmas Fayre and The Melton Mowbray Point to Point collection. The staff, and friends of Warren Pearl already organised a Christmas Fayre each year. So, in my second week as Centre Fundraiser, I took a stall at the fayre to promote Marie Curie Cancer Care and encourage people to donate for daffodils to plant up in support of the charity. It was a joy working with such an enthusiastic group of people. Charlie Neil, the Midlands TV weather presenter, came to support the event.

After the fayre, I invited Charlie to help plant the first Fields of Hope Daffodil bulbs at Marie Curie Centre Warren Pearl. The children from St Martin's School across the road from the hospice came along to help. The manager at the new Safeway's Store in Solihull responded positively to the letter I sent him on my first day in a new job. After meeting him, he offered the use of the store for Christmas fundraising. Thinking on my feet, as fundraisers do, I said we would organise a 'Wishing Tree' in the foyer of the store throughout December. Jo Bray, an Occupational Therapist in Day Care, had previously told me that the patients would be making Christmas Tree decorations and asked if I was able to use these ornaments. It was a pleasure to do so and became an invaluable tool for the whole of December.

A Christmas tree had been donated by Notcutts Garden Centre and the Volunteer Services Manager, Eric Francis, said he would ask some of the volunteers to help with the collection. The first Wishing Tree in 1992 ran very successfully throughout December. Customers were invited to take a decoration, hang it on the tree, make a wish and if they want to, to donate. This fundraising initiative was so popular that it ran for a further ten years. The Mell Square Management Team in Solihull presented the opportunity to have a stall in Mell Square leading up to Christmas 1992. Sue Bodfish, Betty Drummond (my Mum) and I set up a stall of mince pies and mulled wine to promote the work of and fundraise for Marie Curie Centre Warren Pearl. It was freezing cold!

The first national Marie Curie Cancer Care Daffodil Appeal took place in 1986 with volunteers collecting donations and handing out fresh daffodils. In the Spring of 1993, Chris Seaton and I, together with a trusty team of volunteers, took to the streets in the borough of Solihull with fresh daffodils! We made our base in the empty former Gas Showrooms in Mell Square. The logistics of moving hundreds of boxes of fresh daffodils was not without a challenge! Sally Derry, who was known as Matron, then led by example and took a basket of daffodils and a collection box into Mell Square. The off-duty nurses and staff at WP all helped make the Centre's first

Daffodil Appeal very successful, and we went from strength to strength with an ever-growing number of volunteers.

Meanwhile, immediately after my appointment, the lovely Dorothy Dare (who was on my interview panel) suggested a Daffodil Luncheon. In the Spring of 1993, she and her friends help launch what was to be one of the highlights of our fundraising year. We went from a small venue to what was The Solihull Moat House in Homer Road (now the Crowne Plaza). In 1995, Marie Curie replaced fresh flowers with fabric daffodil pins. Three million were given out and £1.2 million was donated. The appeal continued to grow the daffodil was incorporated into the Marie Curie logo, where it remains today.

Part of my fundraising induction was to go to Marie Curie Centre 'Sunnybank' in Liverpool. I was taken with the purpose-built hospice and always hoped that Solihull would have such a place one day. Wishes can come true! The Fundraising Manager at the Liverpool Marie Curie Centre told me about their 'Fields of Hope' campaign. They worked with a local newspaper to launch and maintain the fundraising. People were invited to make a donation and have daffodils planted in memory of a loved one. In return, the name of their loved one would go on a role of honour in the local newspaper. They had chosen Sefton Park to plant up daffodils giving the park a much-needed lift.

I was suitably enthused to adopt this fundraising idea but Brueton Park in Solihull was well kept and certainly did not need a lift. Undaunted, I visited Solihull Parks Department Manager, Mr. Alan Furness-Huson and our Fields of Hope Campaign was born. Fundraising grew and diversified, as community fundraising across the UK was established, and partnerships with major companies were developed.

Our Centre Fundraising team grew when Sue Noone joined. She worked with the volunteers and co-ordinated the placement and collection of our Marie Curie collection boxes throughout the borough of Solihull. In the summer of 1993 Chris, Sue and I worked with the Lions when we entered a Carnival Float to promote Marie Curie Centre Warren Pearl. Our families volunteered to support this venture and, indeed, many more activities. We were so blessed to have the support of Notcutts Garden Centre, and our trusty volunteers to be able to win a prize for our float at Solihull Carnival.

As we worked with local companies, schools, and the local media, the income grew, so it was identified that we needed a full-time finance person to deal with the financial administration and banking. The first charity shop for WP opened, in Knowle, on 7 November 1994 (Marie Curie's birthday). When Marie Curie Memorial Foundation became Marie Curie Cancer Care in October 1995, the temporary WP fundraising shop in Knowle closed and made way for the Marie Curie Shops Department to launch and customise the super Marie Curie Charity Shops throughout the borough of Solihull.

The Daffodil Campaign

My first visit to Day Care, during my induction week, was very special as I got to meet the patients. I remember one patient, a woman called Evelyn, in particular. She told me about her niece Claire at Bradford University, who, with her friends, had offered to help with fundraising. She was planning to use Evelyn's daffodil-yellow car to do a collection from Bradford to Solihull. I was invited to join the patients, Day Care staff and volunteers sitting together in the lounge area. The Occupational Therapist, Jo Bray, asked everyone the question: "What is the best thing that has happened to you this week?" Everyone, with the exception of Evelyn, had a story to tell. She was feeling a little low and felt she had nothing to contribute until I reminded her of Claire's kind offer to support fundraising. Evelyn soon brightened and was happy to tell everyone about her lovely niece. The power of positive thought.

Claire did indeed support Daffodil Day 1993 but, instead of using her Aunt Evelyn's daffodil yellow car, used a Land Rover Defender vehicle. The people at Land Rover were happy to supply Defender vehicles and volunteer drivers to support this fundraising initiative. We had collections all over the Metropolitan Borough of Solihull and had teams of collectors on the streets, in supermarkets, and at Birmingham Airport (which is in the Metropolitan Borough of Solihull). We also had co-ordinators to supply empty boxes and bring in the full collection boxes to the hospice where there was a fantastic team of counters.

When the banks were open, the counted money was banked and when the banks were closed, we had the support of a company who allowed us free use of their safe. As the money was counted, checked and placed in sealed bags this was the safest method of storing the collection money until the banks were open.

Our Daffodil Campaign was able to go from strength to strength thanks to the wonderful support of our enthusiastic staff and volunteers.

What do daffodils symbolise?

Daffodil flowers begin to pop up when winter ends. They are a symbol of spring and symbolise new beginnings and rebirth. They are a positive, life-affirming symbol, with a bright and joyful yellow colour. Daffodils are strong, resilient flowers that pop up year after year. Some people choose to plant daffodils in memory of their loved ones. This can bring reassurance and comfort.

The Fields of Hope Campaign, for Marie Curie Centre Warren Pearl, was an idea from my Liverpool fundraising colleagues which was adapted to suit the Metropolitan Borough of Solihull. When I returned from Liverpool, I met Alan Furness-Huson, Solihull Parks Department Manager, it was the beginning of a very special friendship.

I will always treasure the memory of meeting this delightful man. He was very enthusiastic about the idea of a Fields of Hope Campaign for Marie Curie Centre Warren Pearl. There was no park in Solihull at the time which would benefit from millions of daffodil bulbs being planted in the one place. Alan suggested that Solihull Council commemorate all of their daffodil planting, within the Metropolitan Borough of Solihull, to Marie Curie Centre Warren Pearl.

The next step was to ask for the support of a local newspaper. I visited Angela McLean, Editor of the Solihull Times, and she was so inspired by the work of the WP that she agreed to have a 'Roll of Honour' in the newspaper each week inviting people to make a donation, in memory of a loved one, and in return daffodils would be planted in the Metropolitan Borough of Solihull and the name of that loved one would go on the Roll of Honour. As we had the magnificent support of Solihull Council, we were able to pledge that for every 50p raised, a daffodil bulb would be planted in the Borough.

The Fields of Hope Campaign went from strength to strength. Alan Furness-Huson and Angela McLean continued to support Marie Curie Centre Warren Pearl; they even attended our Daffodil Display Award Luncheon each year and judged the display entries. The campaign was so successful that subsequent editors continued to support Marie Curie in the same way.

Millions of daffodils, commemorated to Marie Curie, were planted throughout the Metropolitan Borough of Solihull, and they appear each year. If you are fortunate enough to drive along the Solihull by-pass in the Spring, you will see thousands of daffodils on each side of the road in a breath-taking display. You will see them all in schools all over Solihull, in verges, and around Birmingham Airport. Indeed, all over the Metropolitan Borough of Solihull in public places you will see the daffodils each spring commemorated to Marie Curie.

In the early 90s, Alan was keen to point out that some miniature daffodils had been planted at the Warwick Road end of Marsh Lane, Solihull. These daffodils are usually the first to appear each year, and they are even more special now as the new hospice is located in Marsh Lane. When you see the daffodils each Spring in the borough of Solihull please think of the patients who have been cared for; who are being cared for; and who, thanks to the support of people like you, will continue to be cared for.

A Typical Fundraising Year

Collection boxes were in place in shops and businesses throughout the year. From late February, all collection boxes were brought in for counting and the Marie Curie Daffodils were in place for the Daffodil Campaign until the end of Spring. The Daffodil Campaign took a great deal of organising and a great deal of volunteer support.

January: Burns Supper
January we would hold a Burns Supper and, as with all of our special events, the Mayor of Solihull was invited. We were thrilled that The Mayor of Solihull Councillor, Les Kyles and his lovely wife Moira, both originally from Scotland, were able to join us at our first Burns Supper. The Shirley Pipe Band made a very special occasion extra special.

February: Pancakes
At the invitation of Mell Square Management, we organised Pancake Races in Mell Square. Teams from local companies took part to compete for the Pancake Race Trophy and raise funds for Marie Curie. Phil Upton, Heart FM Radio Presenter, supported the event.

March: Daffodil Walk
The Sponsored Daffodil Walk in the Spring at Dorridge proved very popular each year. It was organised by Marion and Sid Canning, with help from a wonderful team of volunteers and, of course, the Fundraising Team. At each event the team took the opportunity to promote the next event. Volunteers appreciated that the Fundraising Team worked alongside them and were also giving their time so freely.

Daffodil Campaign - now called the Great Daffodil Appeal.
The Daffodil Campaign ran through out the Spring. Volunteers would take out the fabric daffodil pins to shops and businesses, most of which were supporting Marie Curie with collection boxes throughout the year.

When the campaign was over, all the daffodil boxes were replaced with the collection boxes by volunteers. The counting of all the money took place at the hospice with a trusty team of volunteers helping the fundraising staff. From 1992 – 2004 there was always a 'Daffodil Day' collection on a nominated day. In 2005, the charity used the term 'Great Daffodil Appeal' for the first time.

Daffodil Display Award Luncheon
What started out as a Ladies Daffodil Luncheon grew into a Daffodil Display Award Luncheon. People were invited to create a table display comprising solely or partially of daffodils. The displays were judged on the morning of the luncheon then were used as table arrangements at the luncheon. At the end of the lunch, the winning displays were announced and certificates were presented. A Royal Brierley perpetual trophy was presented to the winner who returned the following year for the next Daffodil Display Award Luncheon. This event was well supported by individuals, flower clubs and latterly, in a separate section, florists. Tickets for the luncheon always sold out and it was yet another opportunity to promote forthcoming fundraising events.

Daffodil Ball
Our first Daffodil Ball in 1995 was to celebrate the 30th Anniversary of Warren Pearl Marie Curie Centre. It followed the Daffodil Display Award Luncheon on the same day at the same venue – The Solihull Moat House.

The next Daffodil Ball was organised by a Committee of super volunteers headed up by a generous and dedicated Chairman. The Marie Curie Centre Warren Pearl Daffodil Ball, held at the

Birmingham Metropole Hotel at the NEC, started in 1998 Marie Curie Cancer Care's 50th Anniversary. Our first Daffodil Ball Chairman was the wonderful Pam Price. Pam had been involved for many years with the Birmingham Poppy Ball in November and very kindly offered to support our first Daffodil Ball in the Spring.

As a result of Pam's expertise and enthusiasm each Daffodil Ball from 1998 – 2004 was a huge success. Pam passed the mantle of Chairman over to Kate Parkin. Vivian Moulder then took over from Kate. Georgina Sapcote took over from Vivian and remained Chairman for three years.

April: Daffodil Concert
We were delighted to welcome a choir from Ystrad Mynach, Mid Glamorgan. It just so happened that Sally Derry's brother was in the Ystrad Mynach Male Choir as well as her nephew. The choir sang for the patients before going over to St Martin's School Hall for the Concert.

I asked Gwyneth Morgan, our Education Tutor at the time, to help me with a welcome speech in welsh. Gwyneth asked for her Mum's help and I wrote it down, phonetically of course. I delivered the welcome speech in my best welsh accent only to find that the only person who spoke welsh was, indeed, Sally's nephew! They appreciated the gesture though. We appreciated the choir singing to the patients, then providing us with a wonderful fundraising opportunity.

May: Melton Mowbray Point-to-Point
From the early 1950's, the Matron of Warren Pearl was invited to Melton Mowbray Point to Point to present the trophy to the winner. Each year staff were encouraged to accompany the Matron and take a collection at the Point to Point. Who, at the Point to Point, could resist a nurse in uniform, or indeed a volunteer with a Marie Curie sweatshirt on when taking a collection for charity?

One nurse collected a great deal of money and certainly put the fun in fundraising! The very attractive Janet Williams put her heart and soul into fundraising on the day of the Races and there were no holds barred! She even went to the Jockey's Changing Rooms and, from what I've heard they were very pleased to see her! A coach party was organised and the off-duty staff and volunteers along with the newly appointed fundraiser went for a day at the races! The tradition endured the fun ensued.

June & November: Fertile Minds Summer & Winter Quiz Evenings
The title of the quiz night was chosen because the venue was always the local garden centre restaurant. There was always much rivalry competing for the honour of holding the Fertile Minds Quiz trophy. Some teams took the competition very seriously, and all appreciated the skill of our volunteer Quiz Master Brian Hilson.

All Year Round: Schools Fundraising
We were blessed to have the support of local schools. Primary and Senior Schools did their own fundraising to support the hospice and still do. We went into schools to tell them all about Marie Curie. We also took something to the Primary Schools which the children, teachers, and volunteers really enjoyed - Teddy Races.

Children were invited to bring their Teddy Bears to school and get sponsored for the teddy to take part in the race. On the appointed day a 'Marie Curie Nurse' came with a stethoscope to examine the teddies to see if they were all fit for the race. Of course, they all passed fitness! The children received a badge the teddies received a sticker and they were all winners.

Daffodil Bulb Planting

In return for the kind support of the schools, we returned in the Autumn with some donated daffodil bulbs to be planted in the school grounds. It was always good to return to the school after all the splendid fundraising for Marie Curie.

December: Carol Singing Marathon

We invited choirs, clubs, and schools to take part each December in a Carol Singing Marathon in the Christmas setting of Notcutts Garden Centre. Each group sought sponsorship to sing for an hour throughout the day so there was continuous carol singing. It was a fun event enjoyed by all.

Wishing Tree

The Wishing Tree took pride of place in Safeway's Foyer throughout December. Shoppers were invited to take a decoration, hang it on the tree and, if they wish, make donation. The collection was very successful.

Tree of Lights

Sue Noone was visiting Newcastle when she noticed a collection was being taken at the foot of a Christmas Tree adorned in lights. She discovered that people had sponsored a light in memory of a loved one.

I approached Solihull Council to seek their help and they came up trumps with advice and support. Woods of Shirley donated the huge Christmas Tree a donation was made to purchase the weatherproof lights and then the donations poured in when people sponsored a light in memory of a loved one. We invited the Mayor of Solihull to switch on the lights a special service. The patients who were well enough to go to the window enjoyed hearing the carol singing and watching the lights being switched on.

This event created lots more administrative work for my hardworking team but, cheerful as ever, they kept on top of all the work and made sure every donor received a Tree of Lights Certificate and an invitation to the switching on ceremony. There were lots of other events, activities all of which involved the support of our wonderful team of volunteers and the generosity and support of companies and businesses throughout the Metropolitan Borough of Solihull.

Marie Curie

Marie Curie's life as a scientist was one which flourished because of her ability to observe, deduce and predict. She is arguably the first woman to make such a significant contribution to science. Marie Curie the charity is proud to be named in honour of her, and I am proud to have worked for such an amazing charity. Some of my time was spent giving talks to various groups and I would always include information about Marie Curie the Scientist. I therefore feel that I should devote a chapter to this amazing woman.

Marie Curie, née Maria Sklodowska, was born in Warsaw on 7 November, 1867. She was the daughter of secondary school teachers, but sadly her mother died when she was young. Marie received a general education in local schools and some scientific training from her father. She became a governess; reading and studying in her own time to quench her thirst for knowledge, and went on to become a teacher. However, Warsaw University did not accept women at that time, so Marie's sister, Bronislawa, offered her lodgings in Paris with a view to going to University. After moving to France in 1891, Marie immediately entered the Sorbonne University in Paris where she read physics and mathematics.

She met a scientist Pierre Curie in 1894 and married him a year later. Their daughter Irene was born in 1897 and a second daughter Eve arrived in 1904. Pierre and Marie were an inseparable team of researchers. They worked with Henri Becquerel and found that uranium gave off rays something the Curies' could later call radioactivity. Working in a primitive space in the school where Pierre taught, Marie was surprised to find that Pitchblende, a source of Uranium contained two unknown elements that were far more active than uranium. Marie named these elements – Polonium and Radium. Polonium was named after her native country Poland. In 1903 she was awarded the Nobel Prize in Physics; the first woman ever to receive a Nobel Prize. In 1911 she became the first person ever to receive a second Nobel Prize when she was awarded a Nobel Prize for Chemistry.

In 1906 Pierre Curie was awarded a full professorship and position as Chair of Physics at the Sorbonne and Marie was promised a position as Director. However, in April 1906 Pierre was killed when he stepped into the path of a horse drawn carriage. Marie was devastated but her professional life took a different turn when she was offered Pierre's chaired position making her the first woman in France to obtain a professorship and allowing her to both continue her research and support her family financially.

She went on to work with her daughter Irene (who later earned her own Nobel Prize in Chemistry) during World War 1 to establish mobile x-ray services and train workers to perform x-rays on the battlefield. It was not until the 1920's that the health hazards of radium emerged. Eventually Marie Curie was diagnosed with pernicious anaemia, caused by years of exposure to radiation. Marie Curie died on 4 July 1934 and was buried in the Paris suburb of Sceaux where her in-laws and Pierre lay. On 21 April 1995, on the orders of French President Mitterand, Marie and Pierre Curie were reburied in the Pantheon, the Paris mausoleum reserved for France's most revered dead. Marie Curie was the first woman to be awarded a place in the Pantheon for her own achievements.

One never notices what has been done, one only sees what needs to be done - Marie Curie.

Dame Cicely Saunders

When talking to my former colleagues at Marie Curie about the idea of writing *My Marie Curie Journey*, Jackie Campbell said if you are writing about our hospice your story must include something about Dame Cicely Saunders. So, to keep my promise, here is a brief biography about this very special woman.

Cicely Saunders was born on 22 June 1918 in Barnet, Hertfordshire. She trained as a nurse, a medical social worker and finally as a physician. Involved with the care of patients with terminal illness since 1948, she lectured widely on this subject, wrote many articles and contributed to numerous books.

Dame Cicely founded St Christopher's Hospice in 1967 as the first hospice linking expert pain and symptom control, compassionate care, teaching and clinical research. St Christopher's has been a pioneer in the field of palliative medicine, which is now established worldwide. Through her single-minded vision, and the clinical practice and dissemination of her work through St Christopher's teaching and outreach, Dame Cicely revolutionized the way in which society cares for the ill, the dying and he bereaved. Her vision to establish her own home for the dying was underpinned by her religious faith. She had initially thought of creating an Anglican religious community but broadened her vision so that St Christopher's became a place that welcomed staff and patients of any faith or none. However, Cicely's strong Christian faith was a fundamental factor in her commitment to the dying and remained an anchor throughout her life.

Dame Cicely is recognized as the founder of the modern hospice movement and received many honours and awards for her work. She held more than 25 honorary degrees, from the UK and overseas. Awards included the British Medical Association Gold Medal for services to medicine, the Templeton Prize for Progress in Religion, the Onassis Prize for Services to Humanity, The Raoul

Wallenberg Humanitarian Award and the Franklin D. Roosevelt Four Freedoms for Worship Medal. Dame Cicely was made a Dame of the British Empire in 1979 and awarded the Order of Merit in 1989.

Dame Cicely Saunders recognized the inadequacy of the care of the dying that was offered in hospitals. So often, patie nts and families were told that there was nothing more that could be done, a statement that Dame Cicely refused to accept. Throughout her time at St Christopher's her watchword was "there is so much more to be done."

Dame Cicely died on 14 July 2005 in St Christopher's Hospice. Marie Curie Nurse, Sylvia Flanner, represented Marie Curie Centre Warren Pearl, when she attended Dame Cicely's memorial service with her husband John. Dame Cicely Saunders and Marie Curie were probably the most influential female figures of 20th Century with a similar attitude to their work.

Our Volunteers

With so many people helping in the hospice it was necessary to have the duties coordinated. Eric Francis was the first Volunteer Manager and when he retired the post was job-shared by John Bendell and Jeff Sutton. Nearly 200 volunteers supported the day to day operations of WP. During my time at the centre the youngest volunteer was 16 and the oldest was 82 and the common thread was that they were all prepared to make a regular commitment of their time.

Duties ranged from driving, helping in the Day Care Unit, reception, serving patients drinks or meals, staff the centre shop, sewing, gardening, clerical work etc. Some of these people also helped with fundraising too and brought our numbers up to in excess of 200 fundraising volunteers.

As a group of staff and volunteers working together, we always felt like one big family. We were always heartened by the hundreds of volunteers who give so freely of their time to enhance the quality of the services provided for the patients and for so enthusiastically supporting the fundraising.

Volunteer Evenings

There were numerous volunteer evenings held at the hospice and the catering team did a magnificent job providing buffets to thank volunteers within the and help fundraise. However, as the fundraising volunteer support soon became so large it was sensible to look for an alternative venue. Thanks to the generosity and kindness of the Manager at Notcutts Garden Centre in Shirley the Fundraising Volunteer evenings were held in the Garden Centre Restaurant.

We held a volunteer evening each year to thank everyone for the support we had received and to tell them about the support we needed for the following year. The fundraising team were frequently congratulated on the way they showed their appreciation to volunteers and, indeed, the innovative themed fundraising evenings. The themed fundraising evenings were particularly well received. There were two themed evenings based on popular television programmes: *Who wants to be a Millionaire* and another called *Stars in their Eyes*.

For the *Who Wants To Be A Millionaire* volunteer evening the fundraising team were quizzed by me as I took the Chris Tarrant role and told they had three life lines; phone a friend, ask the audience and fifty-fifty. The volunteers were asked to participate and some were selected to be 'phone a friend' and all others took part in the raising of hands for ask the audience. The quiz master selected the 'fifty-fifty' questions. The questions would all be based on the achievements and activities of the fundraising team over the previous year.

For *Stars In Their Eyes,* I took the part of Matthew Kelly. We chose specific volunteers to be involved. For example, Marion Canning had been a wonderful Toastmaster at all of our special events and she had also set up a fundraising walk each year. We then chose a member of the fundraising team to be interviewed. Maybe Sue would come forward and I would ask "So Sue, who are you going to be tonight?" Sue would answer, "Tonight 'Matthew' I am going to be Marion Canning"

Then the real Marion Canning would come forward and I would say "What a transformation! You really look like Marion Canning! I understand you have been involved with Marie Curie Cancer Care as a Toastmaster and Walk Organiser. Please tell us all about it."

Prior to these themed presentations we, as the fundraising team, would just make a business-like presentation explaining the events and the money raised and asking for more help.

Marie Curie Centre Warren Pearl, 911-913 Warwick Road, Solihull, West Midlands

Marie Curie Centre Warren Pearl, 911-913 Warwick Road, Solihull, West Midlands

Sally Derry - Matron/Centre

Ellen Ralph - Unit Sister

Kay Horton - Unit Sister

Laura Joy - Unit Sister

Sarah Clemett - Unit Sister

Jenny Royston & Janet Williams - Nurses

June Audley - Nurse

Sylvia Flanner - Nurse

Larry Bland - Nurse

Fran Pearman - Nurse

Penny Moore - Nurse

Beryl Palmer - Nurse

Helen Brown and Janet Williams - Nurses

Jenny Royston and Hazel Craig - Nurses

Linda, Jackie, Melanie, and Laura - Nurses

Sheila Cross, Penny Hewitt and Rachel Knighton - Nurses

Anne Hardie - Home Care Team

Angela Hastwell - Home Care Team

Jane Watson - Home Care Team

Linda Bailey - Home Care Team

Chris Cheadle - Home Care Team

Jayne Taylor - Home Care Team

Mary Fisher, Charm Kelso, and Chris Cheadle

Physiotherapists:
Nikki Goodyear, Marion Dowding,
Jackie Millichap, Christine Brown,
Linda Thompson and Claire Pritchard

Nikki Goodyear - Physiotherapist

Cathy Gurney - Bereavement
Services Co-ordinator

**Occupational Therapists/
Day Centre Manager**
Jo Bray; Penny Hewitt; Fiona Dawes;
Jackie Erskine and Shirley Hanlon

Staff Nurses:
Louise Hathaway; Alison Meakin;
Rachel Lockwood

Jo Bray - Occupational therapist

Sue Scott - Social worker

Social Workers:
Sue Scott; Sally Brennan

Day Care Staff & Volunteers
Sarah Whitehouse – Activities Co-ordinator

Claire Evans - Occupational Therapist
Assistant

Samantha Cox – Occupational Therapist

Joan Griffin – Volunteer

Sarah Whitehouse – Activities Co-ordinator

Samantha Cox – Occupational Therapist

Claire Evans - Occupational Therapist
Assistant

Cathy Gurney – Bereavement Services
Co-ordinator

Shirley Hanlon - Occupational therapist

Sally Brennan - Social worker

Pastoral Services

Back Row L-R: Fr. Ted Simpson; Rev George Hodkinson; Brother Andrew;
Front Row L-R: Renate Wilkinson; Rev Nora Saunders

Gwyneth Morgan - Tutor

Kay Thorman, Staff Development Officer
and Simon Chippendale, Nurse Lecturer

Sharon Hudson -
Staff Development Officer

Dion Smyth – Nurse Lecturer

Christine Lake – Assistant

Lyn Rogers – Assistant

Liz Hancock – Non-clinical Services
Manager

Educational department
Christine Lake - Secretary

Melanie Carthy & Jane Bartholomew
– Staff Development Officers

House Manager
Mike Witts the first House Manager
then John Rogers took the position

Handymen
Tony Pettit and John Quinsey

Sue Skelton - Receptionist

Sue Bodfish - Receptionist /
Volunteer Services Manager

Administrative Team

L-R: Christina Barrett, Dawn Kirsop, Lynn Chamberlin, Sue Skelton & Sue Coleman

Carol Entwistle-Smith - Centre Services Manager

The Pink Team: L-R Jackie Hart, Lorraine While, Janet ???, Linda Newson & Linda Austin

L-R: June Welsh, Linda Kelly, Anita Walters, and Violet Devall

Sue Bodfish, Tony Pettit, and nurses join the catering and the pink team for a fun photo

June Walsh

Catering staff

Linda Kelly

Volunteer Services Department
When Eric Francis retired he handed over to John Bendell. Soon the work became too much for one person so Jeff Sutton joined. When Jeff moved Sue Bodfish and John Bendell worked together.

Eric Francis, John Bendell and Jeff Sutton

Barbara Harwood

Dr Ben Hill

Dr Samira Gabra

Dr Catherine Gearing with Chris Murphy

Dr Sterry

Dr Goode

Dr Ian Morgan

Volunteers:
Here are some of our volunteer collectors who have helped from the very first Daffodil Campaign for Marie Curie Centre Warren Pearl

Volunteers at the Fields of Hope Luncheon 2004

Bill & Gladys Hadley

Marjorie Handley and Hanne Crocker at the Warren Pearl shop known affectionately as "The Kiosk"

Trish Handsley orgnising a breakfast fundraising event at Transco

Joyce (left) & Betty (right) in the Centre's first promotional sweatshirt which they wore at each collection they supported.

Irene Grice a long serving volunteer supported the 'Wishing Tree' initiative and Daffodil Day collection.

The Warren Pearl gardening team

Christmas event Rugby Support Group

Collector Andrew Langstone

Volunteer Evening where staff and volunteers met a man (seated) who met Marie Curie when he was a young boy

Whale Tankers even carried a Marie Curie logo

Chris Murphy and long term supporter Julian Ranson

Claire, Jane & university friends with the Land Rover driver.

Solihull Carnival Float 1993.

Solihull Carnival Float 1994.

The 'Pink' team doing their bit on Daffodil Day.

Chris Seaton, Chris Murphy & Sue Noone.

Anne Williams & Janet Williams (not related!)

Staff Nurse Laura Joy.

Alan Furness-Huson –
keeping the fun in
fundraising!

Burns Night Supper event - Chef and Piper Major

Mayor of Solihull, Councillor Les Kyles, Chris Murphy, Pipe Major, Moira Kyles

Volunteers and Staff with members of the Shirley Pipe Band

Pancake Races - Mell Square, Solihull

Pancake race contestants

Mayor of Solihull presenting the winner Pancake Racers with their trophy

Daffodil Walk Marshalls at a checkpoint

Ystrad Mynach Choir as I attempt to welcome them in Welsh!

In 1993 I was proud to hold the First Daffodil Display Award winning entry and delighted to get a message from Kate Cotton to congratulate the team on the publicity for Marie Curie.

Sue Anderson presenting the Daffodil Display Award shield to the winner of the Florist Section

Exhibition displays

Horace vacated his seat to capture the smiles of the volunteers.

Kate Cotton, from Marie Curie Head Office, with the Mayor of Solihull (1995)

John Adams with his winning entry and his proud mother Rose (1998)

Margaret Rumens & Georgina Sapcote judging the entries

Exhibiton display

Our very own Toastmaster and super volunteer Marion Canning

Horace Gillis our event photographer and super volunteer

Fields of Hope Luncheon 2004
At the Ardencote Hotel in the Warwickshire Countryside.

Daffodil Ball 1995 at the Solihull Moathouse

Daffodil Ball 1998 - L-R ChrisMurphy, Sir Nicholas Fenn and
Pam Price at the Birmingham Metropole Hotel NEC

'Belles of the Ball' -
Sue Anderson &
Chris Seaton

Nurse of the Year
Catherine Le Roy
with her husband

Jenny Neale, Botanical Artist - displaying her creations

Collectors ready to meet Race Goers

Willing hands to help with the collection.

Janet Williams, Sally Derry, Angela Hastwell at Melton Mowbray

Volunteer collectors suitably attired with the new Marie Curie Logo on their sweatshirts. Each year we needed a bigger coach!

Notice the change of logo in the two photos (left and right). No change in the enthusiasm of the volunteers and certainly no change in the splendid care given to the patients and their families.

Brian Hilson our Volunteer Quizmaster and the Quiz marking team

Volunteer crew at the Quiz Night: Phil Barnsley, Chris Seaton, Sheila Hills, Sue Anderson

Winning Team Severn Trent with the perpetual trophy presented by Sally Derry

Winning Team IBM Team with the perpetual trophy

The Kettler Team at the Fertile Minds Quiz

Volunteer Nurse Sheila Cross with the Warren Pearl teddy looking on

Volunteer Nurse Joan Griffin examining the teddies before the race

Christine Lake lending a hand at the Marie Curie Fields of Hope bulb planting at Rugby Cement

Always a fun time – daffodil planting at schools!

Fields of Hope in Stratford upon Avon

Daffodil planting in Rugby

Volunteer Betty Foster with the Manager of The Moat House Stratford upon Avon

Marie Curie Carnival Float

Planting a sponsored sea of flowers around the Marie Curie boat

Warren Pearl Choir supporting the Carol Singing Marathon at Nottcutts Garden Centre with manager Julian Ranson

Getting a lift from some firemen!

Sally Derry receiving a cheque at a 'Night at the Dogs'

Sally's retirement party with family and friends

Sally in conversation with The Lord Lieutenant who presented her BEM medal

Jenny Royston with Rob Bodfish, Alison Meakin to her right and Margaret Buxton to her left at Sally's BEM celebration

Sue Bodfish (red coat) with the walking group

Sally Derry with the walking group

A walk around Kenilworth Castle

This is a photographs of everyone before I got them lost!

By introducing different methods of presentation, it made it more interesting, but just as informative, as previous years.

We were blessed to be based at the Centre, so we saw first-hand the expertise and dedication of all the staff who cared for the patients and supported their families. We were always greatly inspired by the high standard of care and the fact that no-one is complacent about what had been achieved – everyone strives to do more. Marie Curie herself said: "One never notices what has been done one only sees what needs to be done".

Loyal Supporters and Special Friends

We were fortunate enough to gain the support of none other than the Duchess of Gloucester when we opened our new Day Care Unit. I was privileged to introduce Her Royal Highness to staff, patients, volunteers and supporters, as well as my fundraising team.

Don Maclean

Don is an avid supporter of Warren Pearl, and indeed an encourager to me with his wonderful foreword to this book. Don was born in Birmingham and educated at St Philip's Grammar School. He then studied drama at Birmingham Theatre School & modern history at the University of Warwick. A comedian by trade, Don has appeared regularly on TV, in cabaret and theatre all over Great Britain including two London Palladium seasons and six Royal Command Performances.

During the 70s and early 80s he was never off television, he fronted the ever-popular *Crackerjack,* compared *The Black & White Minstrel Show* & was a regular on *Celebrity Squares.* In 1990, BBC Religious Broadcasting invited him to present their 'flagship' programme, *Good Morning Sunday* on Radio 2. His light-hearted approach to religion obviously worked & by the time Don left the show in 2006 two & a half million people regularly tuned in.

Don was made an MBE in the New Year's Honours List 2001, in June 2003 he was invested as a Knight of the Holy Sepulchre at Southwark Cathedral &, in May 2012, Pope Benedict XVI saw fit to confer upon him a Papal Knighthood. Don describes himself as a 'cradle Roman Catholic' having been the only child of a very devout mother & a father who was a member of the Church of Barrow - he only went when pushed. Nowadays he entertains on cruise ships and is still in demand on the after-dinner circuit. Asked when he would retire, Don replied "when people stop laughing!"

William Frederick "Bill" Cotton

During my Marie Curie years Kate Cotton was Director of Administration and Development for the Marie Curie Hospices. Lady Cotton is now Specialists Project Leader for Marie Curie. It was a privilege to welcome both Sir Bill Cotton and Lady Cotton to our Marie Curie Daffodil Luncheon and other special events. I have always been grateful for Kate's encouragement and support. She even entered a daffodil display at our Daffodil Display Award Luncheon 1995.

Bill Cotton, was managerially responsible for many of the BBC's most loved, long-running programmes during the 1960s and 70s golden age of comedy. He was responsible for overseeing the production of a whole series of popular and iconic comedy programmes including *The Morecambe and Wise Show (1968-77)*, *Monty Python's Flying Circus (1969-74)*, *The Two Ronnies (1971-76)*, *Bruce Forsyth and the Generation Game (first run 1971-77)* and *Look: Mike Yarwood (1971-76)*.

Bill was welcomed by a wide range of talent when he became head of BBC light entertainment, then controller of BBC1 and finally managing director of BBC TV, because, unlike many of his predecessors, he was visibly open to drama and light entertainment values. He became controller of BBC1 in 1977 and in 1984 he was promoted to become Managing Director of Television, a role he fulfilled until his retirement from the Corporation in 1988. He was appointed an OBE in 1976 and CBE in 1989.

What made Bill unique was that he revered artists and gave them a chance to breathe - he even gave the puppet Basil Brush his own programme. When he gave the singer Cilla Black her chance, he defended the move by saying he saw her as a version of the British Gracie Fields rather than the American Barbra Streisand. Bill's career did not end with his departure from the corporation. He went on to become presenter Sue Lawley's agent. Indeed, Sue was his only client and they enjoyed many happy meetings to negotiate her terms with the BBC with Desert Island Discs and the Reith Lectures.

Bill was also a golfer and a magistrate. It was while sitting on the Richmond Bench that he met a fellow magistrate, Kate Burgess whom he married in 1990. He was Vice-President of the Marie Curie Cancer Care and received prestigious awards, not least of all a BAFTA Fellowship Award in 1998 and later made a Knight Bachelor for his services to Television Broadcasting and Marie Curie Cancer Care in 2001. This much-loved man died in 2008 and is survived by Kate and the three daughters of his first marriage.

Rosemary Conley CBE DL

It was a delight to welcome Rosemary Conley to our Marie Curie Fields of Hope Luncheon, and receive her support.

Rosemary Conley is one of the UK's leading diet and fitness experts with over 45 years' experience of helping people lose weight and get fit. In 1986 Rosemary discovered a low-fat diet plan, which transformed her body in a way she had never been able to achieve with previous diets. Rosemary put her experiences down on paper and the result was her Hip and Thigh Diet, which was published in 1988 and captured the attention of the nation. This book and its sequel, Rosemary Conley's Complete Hip and Thigh Diet, have sold more than two million copies. Subsequent books and DVDs have seen similar spectacular success, despite being in such a highly competitive market place, with total worldwide sales of over nine million.

From 1993 to 2014 Rosemary and her husband and business partner, Mike Rimmington, operated Rosemary Conley Diet & Fitness Clubs to give additional help, support and motivation to people following her diet and fitness programmes. Just two years after its launch, the British Franchise Association presented Rosemary Conley Diet & Fitness Clubs with its Newcomer of the Year Award and, in 1998, the organisation was presented with the national BFA/Midland Bank Award. In 2002 and 2005, it won the coveted BFA Franchisor of the Year Award.

In 1996 they ventured into magazine publishing and Rosemary Conley Diet & Fitness magazine was launched. From 1996 to 2000 Rosemary was a consultant to Marks & Spencer and helped them to develop their low fat, calorie-controlled food range. Rosemary has presented her own TV series on BBC and ITV as well as appearing on 'This Morning' with Richard and Judy for seven years. She continues to have a high media profile with many regular appearances on national television and Radio. In 2012 Rosemary appeared on ITV1's *Dancing on Ice,* where, at 65 years old, she was the oldest celebrity to make it the furthest in the history of the show – an outstanding achievement. Now in her 70s, Rosemary continues to skate regularly with her professional skating partner from Dancing on Ice, Mark Hanretty.

In 1999 Rosemary was made a Deputy Lieutenant of Leicestershire and in 2001 Rosemary was granted the Freedom of the City of Leicester, the first woman to receive this honour. The following year she appeared on *This is Your Life* with Michael Aspel. In 2003 Rosemary was one of the invited guests at a Reception at Buckingham Palace hosted by Her Majesty the Queen and the Duke of Edinburgh to mark the contribution of 'Pioneers to the Life of the Nation'.

Rosemary Conley was delighted to be made a Commander of the British Empire (CBE) in the Queen's New Year's Honours in 2004, for her *'services to the fitness and diet industries'*. In more recent times Rosemary has turned her interest toward anti-ageing and how the population can to stay fit and healthy in their later years. To this end, she is the UK Distributor for an anti-ageing facial exercise gadget called Facial-Flex® (www.facialflex.co.uk). In addition, Rosemary is Editor-in-Chief of *Life & Style,* an in-house magazine for residents of First Port residential retirement complexes. She has also enjoyed writing her autobiography which she hopes will be published in 2021.

Fiona Castle

We were honoured to have Fiona attend our Marie Curie Daffodil Luncheon during my Marie Curie Years. Fiona was married to Roy Castle, a well-known entertainer who died tragically of lung cancer in 1994. Born in the Wirral, at the age of nine Fiona went to a boarding school in Surrey to study dance and theatre arts. She worked in the theatre as a dancer and singer for seven years before marrying Roy Castle. They were married for 31 years before Roy died, and they had four children. Fiona is now blessed with three grandchildren.

Fiona has written a number of books, including five anthologies of prose and poems, autobiographies and a book on coping with cancer. More recently she has written a book for Global Care, about some of the places where she has worked, on their behalf, in many different countries. She had a regular weekly slot on Premier Radio for five years.

Much of Fiona's time is spent travelling around the UK sharing her story at evangelistic events; speaking at charity events for Hospices, Cancer Research UK Rotary and various church events. She has run the London Marathon twice for Oasis Trust, for which she is a patron, for the first time in 2001 and probably for the last time in 2005! Fiona is also President of Activate; an organisation which encourages Christian women to take God's love into the community, through a wide variety of low-key, friendly events, and seminars, encouraging Christian women in evangelism. She was given an OBE for her work with Global Care and other charities, in 2004.

Notcutts Garden Centre

A great local supporter of Marie Curie Cancer Care was Notcutts Garden Centre. When we started out, Julian Ranson the General Manager said they had previously supported a cancer charity so he was a little unsure whether to support another. However, when I said the Marie Curie logo was a daffodil, he thought the association would be good and, as they say, the rest is history!

Many productive years followed working in association with Notcutts. It was thanks to Julian Ranson that we managed to get such a brilliant float together for Solihull Carnival and won prize money for the charity. Julian challenged me to find a boat which could be a focal point for planting outside the garden centre. I remember saying to him, "Thank you very much we are the furthest point from the sea and you have asked me to find a boat!" However, find a boat we did! It became the 'Marie Curie' and visitors to the garden centre were invited to help plant a sea of flowers and in return, make a donation to Marie Curie Centre Warren Pearl. This was the beginning of our innovative planting and collections at Notcutts.

Our Wishing Tree was donated by Notcutts, our Warren Pearl shop in Knowle was supported by Notcutts, specially themed collections including our Daffodil Day collections were held at Notcutts Garden Centre. Our Volunteer Gatherings were also held at Notcutts. Working alongside Julian, we also ran The Fertile Minds Summer and Winter Quiz each year. The much-loved quizmaster for these events each year was Brian Hilson, a Financial Director of a company in Birmingham and great friend of the fundraising team. Julian was also a judge at our Daffodil Display Award Luncheons and the Fields of Hope luncheons and was a true friend to the charity and all of the fundraising team. I will always be grateful for Julian's loyal and generous support of Marie Curie and for his friendship over the years. It was a partnership which benefitted Notcutts Garden Centre and, indeed, Marie Curie Centre Warren

Pearl. When Chris Seaton and Sue Anderson retired, we held a surprise party at Notcutts. Our wonderful volunteer Phil Barnsley provided the wine and Julian and volunteers dressed the room with balloons and photographs.

Whale Tankers, another local company, was a tremendous supporter of Marie Curie Centre Warren Pearl. The management and staff backed our fundraising events and activities, and even organised a massive Christmas Raffle each year. The idea started when management were given gifts from suppliers so the management team decided to share the gifts with all the staff. They found the fairest way to do this was to have a raffle where everyone purchased tickets and the money went to Marie Curie. Each Christmas I would go to Whale Tankers and draw over a hundred tickets this ensured that the prizes were shared and the money raised went to a really good cause.

Whale Tankers hosted the Marie Curie Cancer Care Ladies Driving Challenge where ladies were invited to get sponsored for driving vehicles they would not normally get to drive. We had fire engines, HGV vehicles, Fork lift trucks, and much more. Another super fundraising event at Whale Tankers was The Dragon Boat Race. On the lake at Whale Tankers, the fancy Dragon Boats arrived and the drummer sat at the front of the boat to beat out the rhythm for the rowers. It was a truly colourful and lively event. It seemed Whale Tankers were one short on their team and seconded me (one short person) on to their team! Being the shortest on the boat I was the nearest to the water and got soaked – twice - but our boat made it to the final!

It was always a pleasure to visit Whale Tankers and, since retirement, a delight to receive a Christmas message from Mike Fisher. As Chairman of Whale Tankers, Mike has set up a website in support of Marie Curie. www.poeticexpressions.co.uk

Giltspur Exhibition Centre

When I took up the post of Fundraising Manager, for Marie Curie Centre Warren Pearl, I was directed to a company at the NEC called Giltspur. The company, with quite a few name changes, supported the charity for many years. They came to our Daffodil Display Award Luncheon and dressed the venue as well as providing a judge from their floral department.

The Daffodil Ball, The Daffodil Display Award Luncheon and Fields of Hope Luncheon benefitted from this company's magnificent contribution. The floral department brought magnificent displays to each of our events and each venue was beautifully transformed. They also donated table arrangements for the Daffodil Ball and where appropriate, following the events, they would take the displays to the hospice for the benefit of the patients. The name of this company changed from Giltspur to Giltspur Show Props, then to P&O Exhibition Services to Melville Floral Services but the one thing which remained constant was their generous support.

There were even more events and activities all of which involved the support of our wonderful team of volunteers and the generosity and support of companies and businesses throughout the Metropolitan Borough of Solihull. There was a great deal of work, behind the scenes, to enable the events and activities to run smoothly. I was truly blessed to have an efficient, caring, hardworking and fun-loving team. It was a privilege to work with my team, the staff at Warren Pearl and indeed all of our volunteers and corporate friends and supporters. We were so fortunate to be based at the centre, so we saw first-hand, the expertise and dedication of all the staff caring for the patients and supporting their families. We were always greatly inspired by the high standard of care and the fact that no-one is complacent about what had been achieved – everyone strives to do more.

Botanical artist Jenny Neale, supported our Daffodil Display Award Luncheon by donating her painting of four daffodils and a volunteer donated a poem to go with the painting. A printing company very generously gave a discount for printing copies of the painting. Jenny signed the limited-edition prints sold at the Daffodil Luncheon. Don Maclean supported our Daffodil Luncheon, on his birthday, at the Solihull Moat House, Homer Road.

Here is the Poem:

The first daffodil is full of love
The second is full of hope
Within the third there is a prayer for strength that you will cope
The fourth daffodil is full of hope and light that God's love will surround you and guide you through the night

The Heart of Warren Pearl

"Many people will walk in and out of your life, but only true friends leave footprints in your heart."
Eleanor Roosevelt

Marie Curie Walking Group

The Marie Curie Walking Group in Solihull was formed by Sally Derry, Sheila Cross and Sue Bodfish for retirees, staff and families. You will remember some of the names from the chapter on Staff.

Here I would like to introduce the eclectic group known as the Marie Curie Warren Pearl Walking Group; Sally Derry, Sue Bodfish and John Bendell are no longer with us but their memories remain. Sheila Cross, Janet Williams, Jenny Royston, Jackie Campbell, Joan Griffin, Marion Dowding, Alison Meakin, Fran Pearman, Jane Bartholomew, Margaret Buxton, Christina Barrett, Renate Williamson, Cathy Gurney, Shirley Hanlon, Angela Hastwell, Mary Bendell, John Bendell, Rob Bodfish, Christopher Murphy, Les Drummond and me Chris Murphy.

Each month, a member of the group organises a local walk. The length of the walk has, over the years, got considerably shorter, and the walk starts and finishes at a feeding and watering hole! Our walking group has got smaller as some have moved, some have encountered walking difficulties (so only join us for lunch), others are no longer with us but are fondly remembered.

On one occasion when it was my turn to organise a walk, I chose a route which I thought I knew well but, alas, I got everyone lost! This would not have been so bad if dear John Bendell had not been in so much pain with a bad back! I was so distressed to have got everyone lost and to see John lying on the ground to ease the pain in his back. In my anxiety I knocked on the door of a cottage to ask for some assistance with directions but no-one was in. I said a

53

prayer then turned to my dear friend, Chris Seaton, and asked her to pray. I then decided to go out into the road and flag down the first car to appear. The first driver to appear was, in fact, my husband Chris returning from golf! It was an answer to prayer! Chris then drove John and a few others back to the watering hole where we left our cars. He then returned to collected everyone else. He was pleased to be given the title 'Knight in shining armour', but he did not accept our invitation to join us for lunch.

We have enjoyed many walks over the years and, indeed each other's company. Those of the group who still walk find that retirement keeps them busy! I asked some of the walking group, former colleagues and volunteers to contribute to this section of the book with their memories of working at Warren Pearl.

Chris Seaton

In 1993 Chris Seaton came to work with me, as my part time secretary, and became my full time, very special friend. Not only did Chris make a difference to the workload, with her computer skills and warm and friendly nature, but she also led me to the Lord. I always believed I was a Christian and when the subject arose in our compact office, I had all the secular answers to hand. Unbeknown to me, Chris was praying in that office and then invited me to her church. It was a charismatic church and, at the time, I felt this was not for me. However, I said to God if this is about you – I'll be back!

Fourteen years later, I was still doing a forty-mile round trip to go to that church. I know that you don't have to eat good food to survive but you do need the right nourishment to be healthy. You don't have to go to church but if you find the right church it certainly nourishes you! I most definitely benefitted from that early nourishment. My faith has helped me through some difficult times in my life and I was blessed to work in a Christian office and I was blessed to work with a Christian team. We were, and still are, a team of friends attending family events, birthdays, wedding and

54

funerals. We all have grandchildren now to keep us busy, but we do get together from time to time to, again, enjoy each other's company. Like many people, I have been blessed to call Christine Mary Seaton my friend. She has a personality which shines and draws people towards God.

Sheila Hills

When Sheila Hills came to work in the Fundraising Department as Finance Officer, she was Sheila Swarbrick. Her fundraising colleagues were delighted to attend her wedding to John Hills and help with planning of what was a lovely day for two lovely people. Chris and David Seaton put their hearts into making the day a success and it certainly was. My husband, Chris, was pleased to be chauffeur.

When asked about our time at Warren Pearl, Sheila wrote: "I remember thinking when I started at Warren Pearl, in fact I always felt, it wasn't just a 'job', but you were doing it to help other people. For that reason, you cared about the job while carrying it out. As I was handed money sometimes by the people who had lost a loved one, it could be upsetting as sometimes the pain was so visible and they would tell you about a loved their loved one they had lost.

My own husband passed away to cancer three years ago so it all seems more relevant to me on how they were all feeling. It was nice to know that the money would be spent on items that would make patients' lives more comfortable. Not all our patients were in the hospice but were at home. I was always grateful to the volunteers that stood for ages collecting money in tins for Warren Pearl. I was also grateful to the volunteers who would come into the office and help count money from the tins. The staff felt in a way like a family with a common cause, and very friendly.

Sally Derry, Matron, visited her patients every day on the wards and everything run like clockwork when she was in charge. The job was also more interesting than most as we would organise an annual lunch, a Ball and be involved in other fundraising events. I particularly enjoyed the Christmas Tree lights event. When people in the community could pay to have a light put on the Christmas Tree in memory of someone they had lost. The tree was outside at the front of the Hospice to raise money for Warren Pearl.

The patients could look out of the windows and see the tree plus hear the Christmas carols being sung by people who came along on the day to enjoy and take part, plus everyone could enjoy the tree when they walked past. In March we would have "Daffodil Day". People everywhere gave money by buying a Daffodil which would raise lots of money to help other people suffering from cancer. It was such a busy time for me counting and banking all the money raised in our community. I had lots of help and was very grateful for it."

Sue Anderson who I called 'my style guru' because she always looks so stylish, wrote: "I have very many happy memories of Warren Pearl. Loved working with a great team of people, including interacting with some very special volunteers. I think my favourite event was the planning and execution of Daffodil Day. Such a buzz, everyone involved showing such dedication. Particularly remember the one when Michael and David helped out. They were so fast at counting money and thoroughly enjoyed lending a hand. The beautiful garden created with the help of volunteers also comes to mind. A peaceful, tranquil place used by patients and staff alike. Teddy races were fun. The schools really got involved."

Sue went on to talk about her favourite anecdote which needs a little explaining. Chris Seaton had, and still has, a lovely way of saying something quite innocently which had a double meaning. Filing was never the most popular job in our office but a necessary one. One day, Chris was very pleased to get a lot of filing done and happily announced: "I am so pleased, I got to P in the filing cabinet". Sue went on to say she "loved job sharing with that very special lady". This leads me on to another special lady.

Sylvia Flanner

Chris Seaton introduced me to Sylvia and her husband John at church. It was an absolute joy and privilege to be part of John and Sylvia's Home Group. Sylvia always had time for people. She was a good wife, good mother, good grandmother, good friend, and was a good Marie Curie nurse. She was the woman behind her husband the inspirational and motivational speaker John Flanner MBE.

Sylvia inspired and motivated in her own right. Despite suffering severe health problem, leaving her bed-bound, Sylvia enthusiastically talked about her time as a nurse at Warren Pearl. When I went to interview Sylvia for this book, it was a joy to see the face of this amazing woman light up when reminiscing about the joy of working at Marie Curie. Despite suffering dementia, the stories and anecdotes just kept coming.

The Interview:

Some of the things Sylvia talked about I already knew but it was good to hear the story from her perspective. One such story is about a patient who was an avid Birmingham City supporter who was nursed by Sylvia, an avid Aston Villa supporter. When it comes to caring for patients all such rivalries are put to one side. Sylvia got in touch with Birmingham City manager and arranged for two City players to visit the patient. Paul Devlin and Curtis Woodburn arrived and made their fan very happy. They brought the Blues strip with them and even had a photograph taken with June from the kitchen.

Sylvia went on to talk about another occasion when she and nurse Larry teased the patient by taking the Birmingham City duvet cover off and putting it to one side saying it was to go in the rag bag. The patient enjoyed the Aston Villa fans joke and enjoyed seeing his Blues duvet cover going back on his duvet! Sylvia then remembered a patient called Dennis, another Blues fan; his Mum was a volunteer on reception. Sylvia told me that Nurse Sheila Cross made home visits to Dennis.

Sylvia smiled when she thought of Nurse Larry Bland because, at the time, Larry was the only male nurse and the other nurses really enjoyed Larry being on duty. Sylvia told me the nurses would send the message around "Larry's in today," and they would ask "Cashmere coat or biker leathers?" Apparently, the patients loved to see him in his leathers. They even asked for their hair to be done when they knew he was coming in.

Everyone was fond of Larry and I was surprised to learn that he went into nursing late in life as he originally worked or Findus Frozen Food company. Larry was meant to be a nurse with his warm gentle nature. Sylvia said there was a patient who needed to be moved and Larry said, "If you are happy, we won't move her on a sheet I will carry her." She was very light and was carried so very gently.

Another patient, Sylvia recalled, was worried about his dog so arrangements were made for the dog to be brought in. An old bread crate was made into a dog bed and the faithful friend slept soundly, as did the patient. Sometime later, whilst shopping in Mell Square, Sylvia met his sisters and daughters. The patients never forgot the kindness shown by the staff at Warren Pearl.

Sylvia's memories were not in any specific order, but she delivered her recollections with a smile and a twinkle in her eyes. She remembered abseiling from the tallest building in Birmingham and getting sponsorship in support of Marie Curie. She laughed when she told me about Sister Sarah Clements abseiling alongside her saying, "Look Sylvia, you can see the people doing their washing up". Pauline Mathias and the church Youth Group went along to cheer Sylvia on. Sylvia did not mention that she had been selected to represent the nursing staff and sit on the top table at our Fields of Hope Luncheon at the Solihull Moat House but I recall her being totally at ease with the Mayor of Solihull and the other guests and, indeed, making them feel at ease.

Sylvia said that Janet Williams had an expression which really amused her. Janet used to say "What's that got to do with the price of fish?" Sylvia and Janet both had a great sense of humour and certainly brought a lot of laughter.

Sylvia enjoyed telling the story about the advertisement for a Senior Nurse. She and Janet decided to each fill in an application form. Janet's form was sent in as Barbara Windsor the much-loved actress with great assets and Sylvia completed her form as Cynthia Payne the notorious woman of the night! The then new Centre Director, Ian Cartlidge, entered into the fun by sending a letter to 'Barbara Windsor' and 'Cynthia Payne' inviting them to attend an interview at the Indian Restaurant where the Staff Party was being celebrated.

So, Janet aka 'Barbara', and Sylvia aka 'Cynthia' both dressed appropriately for the interview much to the hilarity of all at the Staff Party. Sylvia admitted her outfit was far more outrageous than Janet's. Sylvia had gone to a lot of trouble to ensure that 'Cynthia' had all the accessories attributed to her. There was much laughter when Ian read out the section on the application form listing the experience and skills Barbara and Cynthia could offer! The next day, at the hospice, there was even more laughter when Janet and Sylvia told everyone that Brother Andrew, one of the Chaplains of the hospice, walked 'Barbara' and 'Cynthia' home (looking very much like pastoral work!)

The Nursing team brought joy to the patients and joy to each other when they were socialising. Sylvia recalled the time when some of the off-duty nurses had met for a meal together in a local restaurant and a very handsome man came over and kissed Sylvia before he left. The nurses were keen to know who the handsome fella was and asked if John knew about him. At the end of the meal when it was time to pay, the restaurant owner said that the bill had been settled by the man who kissed Sylvia. The nurses were astounded at the generosity of this young handsome man. Sylvia and John were not surprised as they had known the kind and generous Andrew Lockington for some time when they were at the same church together. Andrew, of course, was well aware of the kindness of Sylvia and John over the years long even before Sylvia worked at Warren Pearl.

Sylvia talked about applying for a nursing post at Warren Pearl and on her successful appointment Sally Derry said, "Be careful you don't give your heart away, it will get broken". However, as we all know, when you put your heart into your work there is a distinct chance of getting it broken.

Sylvia showed great love and care to all the patients but there was one who resonated with her. A 27-year-old model who had great spirit. Sylvia recalled seeing her in red silk pyjamas enjoying a rum and coke and a packet of salt and vinegar crisps. The patient returned home for a while then when she needed specialised care she returned to the hospice. Sally turned to Sylvia and said, "Your friend is back – watch yourself".

Sally was protective of her staff and was concerned about Sylvia getting emotionally involved. It was always difficult not to get emotionally involved with the patients for all the staff but especially for the nursing staff. Of course, everything was done, as with all the patients, to give her the best quality of life for the life which remained. Sylvia attended her funeral at St Alphege Church and remembered the wicker work casket with one rose on the top entering the church to the music of Bob Marley singing *One Love*.

I remember when there was a wedding at Warren Pearl. Sally Derry asked me to contact our good friend Julian Ranson and ask if we could borrow some bay trees to line the corridor which would welcome guests and of course the Bride and Groom. It was easy to explain to our understanding friend that the patient may not even be well enough, or indeed be alive, to attend his wedding. However, positivity reigned. It was really heartening to listen to Sylvia talking about this wedding as she and I remembered that the Registrar was very nervous – more nervous than the Bride and Groom, but was made very welcome and set at ease by all the staff.

The catering staff made the wedding cake and buffet. Sylvia told me that British Home Stores supplied the Bride's wedding outfit. It was a wonderful celebration over a Bank Holiday weekend. The staff even created a 'Honeymoon Suite'. The groom lived longer than originally thought and left some wonderful memories for his loved ones.

Sylvia loved talking about the patients and how special they were to her. The food at the hospice was wonderful but sometimes patients had a craving for something so friends would bring in KFC or fish and chips. Food wasn't just brought in for the patients. One patient wanted a Jacuzzi bath to cool off then have a Baileys and ice. So that is what the nurses provided. Sylvia said that Jenny Royston was on duty one night and called the nurses in to have a break. They found the tables had been set and the patient's husband expressed his gratitude by bringing the nurses a Rogan Josh curry.

Sylvia nursed her own uncle, a singer known to his friends as 'Lunchbox'. He sang to other patients. June, from the kitchen, chatted to him and learned that he was a Desert Rat in WWII. It did not pass Sylvia by that one elderly gentleman had just the bare necessities. Indeed, when he walked outside, he did not have shoes to wear. So, typical of Sylvia, she arranged for this patient to have a new pair of shoes. She smiled when she remembered how delighted he was with his new brown brogues and a copy of the Racing Times under his arm.

One nightshift, it was unusually quiet, so the nurses were able hear all about Staff Nurse Rachel's holiday. She was telling the nurses how wonderful it was but, unfortunately, her dog had scratched some paintwork so she went out and bought some paint to leave it in the immaculate condition in which it was found. As it was such a quiet evening, Nurse Penny disguised her voice and rang Rachel saying, "I am from the Holiday Company and we would like £100 as you left the place in such a mess!" Rachel was a good sport and saw the funny side of the joke.

The centre handyman, Tony, was outside working hard picking up bricks. He came across a Mars Bar on the wall with a message from the nurses: "A Mars a day helps you work rest and play!" (this was an old Mars Bar slogan).

We were blessed with some wonderful doctors at Warren Pearl and Sylvia remembered each one of them. She talked about Dr. Ian Morgan, who at the time was in the Territorial Army, and how the nurses packed up a fun box of messages when he was called to go to Iraq. The box also contained sunglasses, flip flops and sun lotion. Sylvia never told me what was on those messages but I daresay they made Dr Morgan smile!

Sylvia had a way of being able to relate to all people at all levels and in doing so made them feel at ease. She was very impressed by Tom Hughes-Hallett, Chief Executive of Marie Curie Cancer Care at the time. She found him very approachable and his red braces were very much admired.

When Sister Laura Joy got married, she had put stainless steel on her wedding list. The nurses, who had been invited to her wedding, gathered up all the cheap silver platters and created a box of junk which was wrapped in wedding paper. Laura took it all in good part but was absolutely delighted with her real present which was a lovely set of wine glasses.

When Sylvia left the hospice, a lot of people cried. There were more tears in December 2018 when Sylvia Rose Flanner went to the Lord. Her funeral, just before Christmas, was amazing – just as a Christian funeral should be. Sylvia touched the lives of so many people. There will certainly be much joy and laughter in heaven now that Sylvia, the joy bringer, is there.

Sally Derry

Each person when asked about their memories of WP always mentioned Sally Derry. When WP first opened its doors in 1965, it was primarily a Nursing Home for people dying of cancer. When Sally Derry joined Marie Curie her title was Matron. She then became the first Centre Director of Marie Curie Centre Warren Pearl.

The emphasis changed from providing inpatient care for a relatively small number of people to the support of many more patients in their own homes through the Home Care Team and the Day Care Centre. As Centre Director, Sally Derry oversaw everything from finance to the fir trees in the gardens.

In our first WP publication Sally said, "When a person is given the news that they have a serious illness like cancer, it may have an absolutely devastating effect on that person, their family and friends. Our role is to try and make an unbearable situation more bearable for that person and their loved ones. We concentrate on trying to improve the quality rather than the quantity of life and on maintaining hope, whilst helping the patient to achieve realistic goals.

Controlling pain and other troublesome symptoms is one way of improving quality of life, whilst physiotherapy and occupational therapy may help a patient to cope with physical deterioration and increasing weakness. Sometimes all we can do is listen, hold a hand, just be there and perhaps that is more important than anything else.

The courage and determination of patients to keep going in the face of insurmountable odds is a constant source of inspiration to us and we feel privileged to be working alongside them. None of this would be achieved without the hard work and dedication of all the staff at Warren Pearl and the amazing volunteers who do so much to enhance the quality of our work and for whom I have nothing but praise and admiration." Sally's words actually sum up why I needed to write about my Marie Curie Journey.

She was an amazing person both privately and professionally. One of our esteemed volunteers, Horace Gillis, said: "Sally Derry left no doubt that she was Matron but she did have a much warmer and more relaxed side as we found out especially, when later, she became a volunteer herself. I always had a lot of time for her." As, indeed, we all did.

Not long after I started work at Warren Pearl, I was invited to attend a cheque presentation, on behalf of the charity, so I asked Sally and two nurses, Janet Williams and Barbara Harsant, to accompany me. The presentation was to take place at a Dog Racing Evening at Hall Green Stadium. We four laughed about the fact that we were 'going to the dogs!' Far from it! We went from strength to strength.

Sally took a great interest in the fundraising events whether it was presenting a trophy at the Quiz Evenings, making a speech at Concerts, collecting on Daffodil Day or dressed in her finery to attend the Daffodil Ball she did with great enthusiasm. Having a Centre Director with a nursing background meant a great deal to everyone at WP.

I think Sheila Hills, the fundraising Finance Officer, summed it up very well when she said, "Sally Derry, Matron, visited her patients every day on the wards and everything ran like clockwork when she was in charge." She carried out her duties with efficiency and a kind heart and her team followed this example.

When Sally retired, she continued volunteering for Solihull Bereavement Counselling Service and, with Sue Bodfish, set up the Marie Curie Walking Group. Sadly, Sue Bodfish died and Sally and the Walking Group organised a walk called 'Sue's Walk' and planted daffodils en-route in her memory.

In 2013 Queens Birthday Honours List Sally was awarded a BEM for services to the Solihull Bereavement Counselling Service and to the community in Solihull, West Midlands. We had a super celebration at St Helen's Church, where Sally worshipped, and enjoyed seeing Sally being presented with her BEM medal.

In life there are highs and lows. A low point was when Sally arrived at one of our walking group gatherings, of mainly Marie Curie retirees, to announce that she had been diagnosed with cancer. Later that year we all met up for a Christmas lunch and, sadly, it was the last time Sally joined the Walking Group she had founded. Sally Derry died on 1st March 2014. The whole of her working life was devoted to nursing, a large part of which latterly was in Birmingham and Solihull. Her career began with her training at Bart's in London where she received a gold medal for the best examination results in her year. Sally undertook various nursing roles in a number of locations, including a couple of years in Australia.

When she returned to the UK she headed for Birmingham where she became Ward Sister then Nursing Manager in cardiology at East Birmingham Hospital (now Heartlands). She became increasingly interested in and concerned with holistic end of life care, and was something of a pioneer in palliative care as we know it today. She subsequently took on the role of Matron at Warren Pearl. A service of thanksgiving was held at St Alphege Church, Solihull, and the church was full. She was a very special woman and has left some very special memories.

When I decided I would be taking early retirement in 2004 I made sure senior management had plenty of advance notice. During this time fundraising in the Midlands underwent a restructuring. The Fundraising Manager for Birmingham, Sue White, took on the additional responsibilities of managing the fundraising at WP and I became Fundraising Manager for Warwickshire. I still kept in touch with everyone at the Centre and I was blessed to have the continued support of loyal friends: Julian Ranson, at Notcutts, Mike Fisher, at Whale Tankers, and the generous support of volunteer Phil Barnsley as well as many others.

As the fundraising in Warwickshire gathered momentum, more heart-warming stories from the Marie Curie nurses emerged. One nurse told me about a patient who was very weak but her one desire was to attend her son's wedding. So, this Marie Curie nurse, on her day off, assisted the patient with her wedding outfit, provided the transport and escorted her to the wedding ceremony. The patient saw her son married and returned home with the Marie Curie nurse at her side. Stories like this continued to inspire the efforts of the fundraising volunteers.

I was so blessed to be able to keep in contact with my Marie Curie colleagues at Warren Pearl whilst working as a Marie Curie Community Fundraiser in Warwickshire. I was blessed that companies extended their support into Warwickshire, that volunteer Phil Barnsley worked alongside me and supported and enhanced every event and activity. It is good to know that each time the Marie Curie Fields of Hope daffodils appear in Rugby, Stratford upon Avon and Kenilworth, that people are reminded of the wonderful work of the Marie Curie Nurses in the community. Volunteers organising events for Marie Curie always welcomed the presence of a member of Marie Curie staff. From a fundraising perspective it was an opportunity to thank, encourage, and to promote further fundraising events and activities.

In 2004, Lynn Woods took up the Post of Fundraising Manager for Marie Curie Centre Warren Pearl and Birmingham and I attended the last Fields of Hope Luncheon in Warwickshire before retiring later that year. In 2013, Lynn Woods went on to became Fundraising Manager for Marie Curie Hospice West Midlands.

Fond Memories

Janet Williams said she remembered 'going to the dogs' with the new fundraiser, Chris Murphy. It was the first cheque presentation event and I was asked to invite the Matron and some nurses. So, Sally Derry, Janet Williams, Barbara Harsant, and I went along. It was a fun evening but the thing which made us smile was the first involvement with the new fundraiser was 'going to the dogs'!

Janet also recalled how Matron had organised some refurbishment of the old building and all the patients and staff were transferred to Solihull Hospital. Janet, Barbara and I had a preview of the refurbishment and there was much excitement shown by the nurses to have a special bathroom with hoists. Things have come a long way since! Janet was always full of fun and mentioned the Melton Mowbray Point to Point collections and meeting with the jockeys.

Jackie Campbell said that if there is going to be a story about Marie Curie there should be something written about Dame Cicely Saunders.

Horace Gillis volunteered to help our Fundraising Team over 25 years ago and his advice, support and friendship was deeply appreciated and will always be treasured. Horace reflected on the Daffodil Day collection in 1993 in Mell Square, Solihull, handing out fresh daffodils. Then he talked about the warmth and friendship of the team on counting days and enjoying Barbara Barker's rock cakes! Horace even remembered moving from our very small office to a much larger room in 'the turret' on the top floor.

I will never forget Horace helping me set up the systems for the Fundraising Team and producing management information for Head Office. Of course, one cannot talk about our Marie Curie journey without mentioning Sally Derry. Horace said, "she left no doubt that she was Matron but she did have a much warmer more relaxed side as we found out when she became a volunteer herself" Horace, like most of us, had a lot of time for Sally.

Horace talked about Rose and her son John at our Daffodil Display Award luncheon and this prompted me to include a photograph of John with his display and Rose looking on proudly. If John's personality got too noisy, it only took one look from his mother to quieten down! Horace rightly points out that Rose was a delight who accepted John with his problems as if they were the most normal thing in the world. John looked after his Mum as best he could – locking up the house at night, making her early morning tea. He became more independent with her encouragement so that he could live in sheltered accommodation. John was a well-recognised figure in Solihull and Birmingham making his trade mark calls. His attendance at the Tree of Lights, Horace recalls, when he occasionally caused some disruption because he was so excited to see the Mayor.

Horace, and many others, were keen to retain the name Warren Pearl because it reflected affection for the old hospice and the family it was. However, Horace concedes, that not retaining the name was the right decision. He also, kindly, paid tribute to the 'consistently happy and cheerful two Chris's'. Both Chris's retired, but Horace continued to volunteer and was honoured with an invitation to represent the Solihull Hospice at a Reception by the Prince of Wales at Clarence House to celebrate 30th Anniversary of the Great Daffodil Appeal in May 2016. Horace still helps with the Daffodil Collection in the Spring.

Chris Seaton said: "Some of the things that stand out in my memory during my 12 years working in Fundraising at Warren Pearl was, first and foremost, working with such a special team and the lasting friendships we all have. Chris's motto was "let's keep the fun in fundraising" which we certainly did. Sometimes we were on overload with events to organise and deadlines to meet but we all pulled together and had the satisfaction of 'a job well done'. When Chris joined me at Warren Pearl, despite being part-time, she managed to keep the office in good order and support the fundraising events. She very rarely felt overwhelmed but when I asked her about her memories of working at Warren Pearl she said;

"One of my early initiations into my new job was the Fields of Hope Campaign, Chris and I made up the total fundraising team at that time. Chris had arranged and publicised the campaign in the local paper and was out of the office the next day. We hadn't expected such a rapid response from them, but I ended up being inundated with monetary gifts and coupons which, of course all had to balance before presenting to the Centre Finance Manager. I did, at last, emerge from the avalanche! Our Matron, Sally Derry, came in towards the end of the day to calm my frayed nerves. Perhaps this experience led to fundraising having our own Finance Officer."

Chris then recalled some of the memories of her time in Fundraising at Warren Pearl she said, "I particularly loved the primary schools' sponsored teddy races when the children would bring their teddies to be checked before running in their race. Nurse, complete with stethoscope, would give a thorough health check to all teddies and whatever cuddly animal would be in line."

Chris had a great rapport with the volunteers as she recalls: "I loved seeing our helpful, volunteers who were so enthusiastic to support the fundraising. There were many faithful volunteers who

69

supported fundraising for years and we couldn't have managed without them. Gordon Barker was a regular visitor to our office, he would design posters and be back and forth from his home computer to the office on many occasions more than once until the final design was agreed. He loved it!

Horace helped with finance, until we had a Finance Officer, and certainly came into his own on Daffodil Day managing the team of 'counters'. It was a great joy to see him begin to live again after suffering bereavement.

There are of course many other volunteers who would visit and assist us, particularly when we moved from the third floor to the ground floor where we were more accessible. Everyone in the centre, staff and volunteers alike were working to do and be the best they could for the good of those patients and families needing care and support. The nurses were amazing and I certainly felt proud to have worked in the Centre."

The Work Goes On

On 21 June 2013 His Royal Highness, The Prince of Wales, Patron of Marie Curie, officially opened the new £20 million Mare Curie Hospice, West Midlands in Solihull. The hospice is on Marsh Lane, just 500 metres away from the site of the old Solihull Hospice, Warren Pearl.

The new hospice is bigger and its purpose-built facilities will provide services to more patients and their families in Solihull, Birmingham and Warwickshire. I was privileged to have a tour of the hospice and it is most impressive.

There are 24 private and spacious bedrooms, all with en-suite bathrooms as well as direct access to landscaped gardens. A day services unit, which supports twice as many patients compared with the old hospice, offering clinical support, rehabilitation, emotional support, practical advice and complimentary therapies. Outpatient facilities and services enable more patients to remain at home with the best quality of life. There is a rehabilitation room and gym to help patients develop the skills they need to maintain their independence and quality of life. An integrated greenhouse has been built into the hospice, giving patients year-round access to plants and horticulture.

The gardens include two large formally laid out patients' gardens, including a ball fountain water feature, indoor courtyards, a vegetable plot, a long border adjoining the car park, gardens and a beautiful wildlife and pond area at the rear of the hospice. The volunteer gardening team work to provide a peaceful and comforting place for patients, their visitors and staff.

I first met Charlotte Lindley, the Hospice Manager, when our Marie Curie Walking Group called into the hospice restaurant for lunch. Charlotte took the time, in her lunch break, to meet Marie Curie retirees and hear all about our Walking Group. We were all impressed that she was a manager with a nursing background. It was a pleasure to meet Charlotte again and interview her for this book. It was fascinating to hear about Charlotte's journey from her training at Whittington Hospital, North London, to her current role as Marie Curie Hospice Manager.

It was during her time as a trainee that she learned about the work of hospice nursing. Her mentor, had secured a placement in a hospice and Charlotte was impressed with what she heard; it was at that point she knew she wanted to work in a hospice. Charlotte moved to Eastbourne and whilst raising her three children she worked as a bank nurse for four years on a night shift. She was pleased be join the Hospice at Home Team and delighted to be on day work. It was at this point Charlotte decided to take a degree in palliative care and did this whilst keeping up her nursing skills.

Whilst based in the rural environment of Uckfield, Charlotte enjoyed working in a small team providing an integrated nursing service to the local community. As Manager of Hospices at Home, Charlotte covered all sections of the Hospice. At St. Wilfrid's Hospice in Eastbourne, Charlotte was appointed Head of Community Engagement, responsible for all income and raising the hospice's profile. She spent 17 years at St Wilfrid's Hospice and in 2013, her husband's job brought her to the Midlands.
Charlotte applied for a position with Marie Curie Hospice West Midlands, went for an interview two days before her 40th birthday on 24 June, was married in July and started her new job in September 2013. What a year it was for her!

Charlotte became the Help the Services Manager West Midlands, recruiting and training volunteers - a post which she held for four years. She also learned that all her hard work fundraising for St Wilfrid's Hospice resulted in the completion of a new build for the hospice in 2013. Marie Curie Hospice West Midlands was, of course, officially opened by HRH Prince Charles, the Prince of Wales in 2014.

In September 2017 Charlotte was appointed Hospice Manager. She enjoys bringing everyone together and took great pride in telling me about the staff and volunteers at the hospice. In 2019 over 100 volunteers enjoyed attending the Volunteer Thank You Event when they were serenaded by a Ukulele band.

Charlotte said that one of her favourite events was celebrating the Royal Wedding of Prince Harry and Megan Markle. She chose to highlight this event because it brought staff, patients, and volunteers together, something that is very dear to Charlotte's heart.

Whilst at the new hospice, it was a pleasure to catch up with Lynn Wood and hear about the fundraising in 2019. As Fundraising Manager, Lynn now has a team comprising one hospice Fundraising Assistant, and six Community Fundraising Managers covering Gloucestershire, Herefordshire, Worcestershire, Coventry and Warwickshire, West Midlands, South Staffordshire and Shropshire.

The team's task is to raise £1.3 million each year which is achieved by having a structured approach on tried and tested products. It was wonderful to see that one of the tried and tested events remains from the days at Warren Pearl and that is the Tree of Lights. It has the same format as before but has been re-named 'Lights to Remember'. It was a joy to hear that the Volunteer Gardeners did some fundraising to buy a massive tree which has been planted and is now a permanent fixture for this very popular event. Lynn told me that 500 – 700 people attend each year for the switching on of the lights and carol singing.

A great deal of effort continues to go into the Great Daffodil Appeal which runs from February to the end of April followed by the 'Blooming Great Tea Party' summer event and the 'Lights to Remember' in December. These events raise awareness and support thanks to the fundraising groups and key volunteers. The Community Fundraising Managers all have their own targets but all work together for the benefit of the charity. Even after nearly 30 years Team work prevails! As the acronym TEAM spells out; Together Everyone Achieves More!

At the end of Marsh Lane, miniature daffodils were planted by the Metropolitan Borough of Solihull for Marie Curie Cancer Care's first Fields of Hope Campaign in 1993. Remembering that the daffodil is a symbol of hope and when those daffodils were planted it was hoped that Solihull would one day have a new hospice.

New hospice, better facilities ... same amazing care. I am so incredibly honoured to have been a part of the journey. Thank you for allowing me to share it with you.

Look backward with gratitude
Look upwards with confidence
Look forward with hope.

A Word of Thanks

Thank you to all the amazing people I met on my Marie Curie Journey for the happy memories.

Thank you to friends and family for their unfailing support.

Thank you to re:creates for their expertise and patience.

Thank you to Lady Kate Cotton, Fiona Castle, Rosemary Conley and Don Maclean for their enthusiastic support.

Thank you to John Flanner for his encouragement – without which this book would never have been published.